Certificates of Competence

Course	RYA/MCA Coastal Skipper	RYA/MCA Yachtmaster Offshore	RYA/MCA Yachtmaster Ocean
Previous experience & minimum sea time *see note 1*	30 days seatime 2 days as skipper 800 miles 12 night hours *see note 2*	50 days seatime 5 days as skipper 2500 miles 5 passages over 60M, including 2 overnight and 2 as skipper	Ocean passage as skipper or mate of watch
Form of examination	Practical	Practical	Oral and assessment of sights taken at sea *see note 3*
Certification required before examination	Restricted (VHF only) Radio Operator's Certificate First Aid Certificate	Restricted (VHF only) Radio Operator's Certificate. First Aid Certificate	RYA/MCA Yachtmaster Offshore Certificate. Yachtmaster Ocean Shorebased Course Completion Certificate
Minimum duration	6 to 10 hours for one candidate 8 to 14 for two	8 to 12 hours for one candidate 10 to 18 for two	Normally about 1 1/2 hours
Certificate of competence (only obtained by examination)			

1   Within 10 years of examination
2   If you have a Coastal Skipper Practical Course Completion Certificate the seatime requirement is reduced to 20 days (2 days as skipper), 400 miles and 12 night hours
3   Written exam in lieu of shorebased course completion certificate

RYA Sail Cruising and Yachtmaster Scheme

Syllabus and logbook

PENNY HAIRE
RYA Chief Cruising Instructor

D1513594

Photo Credits: Christel Clear, Patrick Roach and Peter Bently.

The RYA is committed to encouraging both women and men to participate in sailing. For clarity only, the text of this logbook is written in the masculine gender eg Man overboard.

Published by
The Royal Yachting Association
RYA House Ensign Way Hamble
Southampton SO31 4YA
Tel: 0845 345 0400
Fax: 0845 345 0329
Email: info@rya.org.uk
Web: www.rya.org.uk

G15 REVISED AND UPDATED 2004

INTERNATIONAL SAILING HANDBOOK	International Sailing Schools Association
LIVRET INTERNATIONAL DE VOILE	Association Internationale des Ecoles de Voile
INTERNATIONALES SEGELHANDBUCH	Internationale Zeilscholen Vereniging
	Internationale Segelschulen-Vereinigung

Contents

| *Indicates a change to the previous edition*

This book is effective for examinations, shorebased courses and practical courses from 1 January 2004

Finding the right course for you

Before taking a course you should look carefully at the experience requirement (see inside front cover) and, if necessary, discuss your level of ability with an RYA Training Centre or your shorebased tutor. The intention of the courses is to improve your ability in the sport and therefore allow you to gain more enjoyment from yachting. Attempting a course above your current level of ability is counter productive and will be of less use to you than one which is realistically pitched at your level.

To select an RYA Training Centre that will meet your needs, visit the RYA website for a list of centres: www.rya.org.uk or call the RYA on 0845 345 0400 for free brochures which list all the shorebased and practical course centres. For centres outside Europe go to www.rya-training.com

RYA Courses

RYA theory and practical courses are run by over 1,100 RYA Training Centres, clubs and adult education centres throughout the UK and overseas.

Shorebased

The shorebased scheme teaches the theory of navigation and seamanship in courses of forty hours duration plus home study; and provides one day courses for the theory and practice of: VHF radio operation, first aid, radar, sea survival and diesel engine maintenance. See page 55 for more information.

Practical Courses

Practical courses take place at sea, usually on five day courses on board a cruising yacht operated by an RYA Training Centre and are structured to provide specific courses from Start Yachting up to Coastal Skipper. See page 7 for more information.

Course Completion Certificates

At the end of your course, the Principal or Chief Instructor will decide whether course completion certificates are to be awarded.

The RYA/MCA Yachtmaster Scheme

RYA/MCA Yachtmaster Offshore qualifications are only gained by practical examination. There is no requirement to take an RYA course before taking the examination - unless you take the exam outside the UK. The examinations are open to anyone with the required experience. Successful candidates will be awarded an appropriate Certificate of Competence. See page 45 for more information.

Certificates of Competence

An RYA/MCA Certificate of Competence is recognised by maritime authorities throughout the world and is often one of the the required qualification options for professional skippers.

Keeping a Log

To participate in the RYA training schemes at any level we recommend that you keep a record of your cruising and racing hours. A validated record of your sailing experience is a useful indicator for the practical courses and absolutely essential to enter for the RYA/MCA Yachtmaster examinations. This book provides log matrices for you to fill in on pages 31 to 43 together with notes about experience and skill levels.

RYA Training Centres

All RYA Training Centres, which may be clubs, sailing schools or sea training organisations, must have qualified staff, suitable boats and adequate safety cover, and should display a Certificate of Recognition specifying the activities for which they are recognised. Recognition involves the school being run by a Yachtmaster Instructor, all skippers being qualified, and the sailing yachts used conforming to the very stringent regulations laid down by the Maritime and Coastguard Agency and the RYA. Commercial school yachts must carry a Small Commercial Vessel Certificate. Centres are also required to carry public liability insurance.

Safety is a priority for the RYA. Each RYA Training Centre is regularly inspected for standards of tuition, facilities and equipment, as laid down by the RYA Training Division.

Learning Resources

The RYA produces a wide range of resources to help you learn.

- course notes and exercises, comprehensive handbooks and topic books

- interactive training CDs for electronic plotting and navigation and seamanship theory

- and a wide range of supporting videos and DVDs.

All these can be obtained through RYA Training Centres, the RYA website or simply phone the RYA and ask for this free catalogue.

Australia
Publications can be obtained from
Boat Books +61 29 439 1133
www.boatbooks-aust.com.au

New Zealand
Publications can be obtained from
Transpacific Marine +64 09 3031 459
www.transpacific.co.nz

All practical courses, other than Start Yachting, are five day courses cruising on board an RYA Training Centre yacht.

You can enter the Sail Cruising Scheme at any stage according to your knowledge and experience; there is no requirement to start at beginner's level.

If you are unsure whether you are Day Skipper or Coastal Skipper standard, it is often easier to let your instructor advise you during your first few days on your course.

Course Requirements

On each course the following requirements must be fulfilled:

- The sea school will be an RYA recognised training centre

- The pupil/instructor ratio must not exceed 5:1.

- The minimum duration for courses above Start Yachting is five days. This may be continuous or over weekends

- Except in exceptional circumstances and for the Start Yachting course, the yacht should not day sail from her home port. The instructor will plan an itinerary taking into account the ability of the crew, the weather conditions and the requirements to cover the syllabus

- The yacht should sail a minimum of 100 miles

- Each member of the crew should experience at least four hours of night watch-keeping

- For all courses the instructor will hold a Yachtmaster Offshore Certificate with a current Instructor's endorsement. Instructors are required to update their qualification every five years

- During the Day Skipper and Coastal Skipper courses, each trainee skipper will be given an opportunity to skipper the yacht under instruction and will receive a full debrief during or at the end of the passage

- During each course the instructor will inform the students of their progress and ensure that everyone is aware of their strengths and weaknesses

Course Completion Certificates

The authority to award certificates of satisfactory completion of practical courses is delegated to RYA Training Centres, which may be clubs, sailing schools or sea training organisations.

Individual instructors not working as part of a recognised school may not run courses or sign the course sections of the the logbook or issue certificates.

Own Boat Tuition

Sailing schools may offer instruction for RYA Certificates in a student's boat. Before doing so however, the Principal must ensure that the boat is in sound condition and is adequately equipped both for safety and effective instruction. There is no requirement for a Small Commercial Vessel Certificate for a boat which is being used for the owner's instruction and that of his or her family or friends.

Competent Crew and Day Skipper/Watch Leader

These two courses are set out in such a way that those who wish to work towards a certificate of satisfactory completion with clubs or members of the Association of Sea Training Organisations may do so over a protracted period. A course for either of these two grades taken on a continuous basis at a sailing school will take about five days.

Both certificates may be awarded irrespective of whether the candidate holds a certificate of satisfactory completion for the equivalent shorebased course. However, the possession of the shorebased course completion certificate will greatly enhance the value of the practical course as the instructor will be able to concentrate on the practical aspects of the syllabus.

Coastal Skipper

This is a course for potential skippers and it is assumed that those attending it will be competent sailors with a good knowledge of the theory of navigation and meteorology, and will already have a level of experience approaching that required for the Coastal Skipper Certificate of Competence (see page 47).

There is not sufficient time during the course to teach the basic skills of seamanship, helmsmanship and navigation, as well as to teach how these skills should be applied by the skipper of a yacht. Students will be assessed during the course and certificates of satisfactory completion will not be awarded to those who:

• are adversely affected by sea-sickness to the extent that their ability to skipper a yacht is reduced to a dangerously low level

• are unable to demonstrate sufficient ability in basic seamanship, navigation and yacht handling to appreciate the technique and skills required of a yacht skipper

• demonstrate a lack of understanding of any part of the syllabus to the extent that it would be dangerous for them to go to sea as the skipper of a yacht

Non-tidal Courses

These courses are specifically designed for yachtsmen and women who wish to sail in the Mediterranean and Baltic Seas. Although included in this logbook, the non-tidal skippering courses are quite separate from those gained in tidal waters. There is no conversion course from non-tidal to tidal. If you have taken a non-tidal course and require a tidal certificate it will be necessary to attend another five day course.

The Start Yachting and Competent Crew Course are the same in tidal and non-tidal waters.

Practical training for the RYA/MCA Yachtmaster Offshore Certificate of Competence

No syllabus is prescribed for a practical course for the Yachtmaster Offshore Certificate. However, training centres may offer courses in preparation for this examination, either to give candidates experience of making longer passages or simply as a refresher course on aspects of yacht handling, navigation and seamanship.

Swimmers

It is strongly recommended that all those participating in the sport of cruising should be able to swim. Non-swimmers will normally be required to wear a lifejacket at all times.

START YACHTING SYLLABUS

This course provides a short introduction to sail cruising for novices. By the end of the course, participants will have experienced steering a yacht, sail handling, ropework and be aware of safety on board.

Holders of a Start Yachting certificate can obtain a Competent Crew certificate by completing a further three days or two weekends of the Competent Crew course.

1 The yacht
* Basic knowledge of sea terms, parts of a boat, her rigging and sails

Instructor's signature

2 Ropework
* Ability to tie the following knots: figure of eight, round turn and two half hitches, bowline

* Securing a rope to a cleat

* Use of winches and jamming cleats

Instructor's signature

3 Underway
* Has experienced sailing a yacht on all points of sail

* Can steer a yacht under sail or power

Instructor's signature

4 Rules of the road
* Can keep an efficient lookout at sea

Instructor's signature

5 Meteorology

- Knows where to obtain a weather forecast

_____

Instructor's signature

6 Man Overboard recovery

- Understands the action to be taken to recover a man overboard

_____

Instructor's signature

7 Clothing and equipment

- Understands and complies with the rules for the wearing of safety harnesses, lifejackets and personal buoyancy aids

_____

Instructor's signature

8 Emergency equipment and precautions

- Is aware of hazards on board a yacht

- Knows the action to be taken in the event of an emergency

_____

Instructor's signature

COMPETENT CREW SYLLABUS

The competent crew course introduces the complete beginner to cruising and teaches personal safety, seamanship and helmsmanship to the level required to be a useful member of the crew of a cruising yacht.

1 Knowledge of sea terms and parts of a boat, her rigging and sails
- Sufficient knowledge to understand orders given concerning the sailing and day-to-day running of the boat

Instructor's signature

2 Sail handling
- Bending on, setting, reefing and handling of sails
- Use of sheets and halyards and their associated winches

Instructor's signature

3 Ropework
- Handling ropes, including coiling, stowing, securing to cleats and single and double bollards

- Handling warps

- Ability to tie the following knots and to know their correct use: figure-of-eight, clove hitch, rolling hitch, bowline, round turn and two half hitches, single and double sheet bend, reef knot

Instructor's signature

4 Fire precautions and fighting

- Awareness of the hazards of fire and the precautions necessary to prevent fire
- Knowledge of the action to be taken in event of fire

5 Personal safety equipment

- Understands and complies with rules for the wearing of safety harnesses, lifejackets and personal buoyancy aids

6 Man overboard

- Understands the action to be taken to recover a man overboard

7 Emergency equipment

- Can operate distress flares and knows when they should be used.
- Understands how to launch and board a liferaft.

8 Manners and customs

- Understands accepted practice with regard to:

  use of burgees and ensigns, prevention of unnecessary noise or disturbance in harbour including courtesies to other craft berthed
- Aware of the responsibility of yacht skippers to protect the environment

9 Rules of the road

- Is able to keep an efficient lookout at sea

10 Dinghies

- Understands and complies with the loading rules
- Is able to handle a dinghy under oars

Instructor's signature

Instructor's signature

Instructor's signature

Instructor's signature

Instructor's signature

Instructor's signature

Instructor's signature

11 Meteorology

- Awareness of forecasting services and knowledge of the Beaufort scale

Instructor's signature

12 Seasickness

- Working efficiency is unaffected/~~partially affected/severely affected~~ by seasickness. (Delete as applicable)

Instructor's signature

Club Sail
Sea School
Est. 1986

13 Helmsmanship and sailing

- Understands the basic principles of sailing and can steer and trim sails on all points of sailing

- Can steer a compass course, under sail and power

Instructor's signature

Club Sail
Sea School
Est. 1986

14 General duties

- Has carried out general duties satisfactorily on deck and below decks in connection with the daily routine of the vessel

Instructor's signature

WATCH LEADER SYLLABUS

The Watch Leader course is conducted onboard a large yacht (over 15m LOA) or a sail-training vessel to teach watch keeping, seamanship and navigation up to the standards required for taking charge of a watch on deck, at sea or in harbour, under supervision of a deck officer. The watch leader syllabus can be conducted in tidal or non-tidal waters.

1 Preparation for sea
Understands & is able to carry out the following duties:

- Secure & stow all gear on deck & below
- Preparation of crew
- Engine, life saving and fire fighting apparatus checks

Instructor's signature

2 Deck work
Can organise a watch to carry out the following duties:

- Sail hoists & sail drops
- Reefing & shaking out reefs
- Prepare, drop & weigh anchor
- Prepare, send & retrieve warps while coming to or slipping alongside
- Mooring to & slipping from a buoy

Instructor's signature

3 Navigation
Is proficient in the following navigational duties:

- Can plot a fix using electronic means
- Knowledge of IALA buoyage
- Maintenance of navigational records
- Use of echo sounder and lead line

Instructor's signature

4 Pilotage

Understands the use of leading lines, clearing lines, transits & soundings

----
Instructor's signature

5 Meteorology

- Knows sources of forecast information

- Can record weather forecasts from radio broadcast sources

Instructor's signature

6 Rule of the road

Has a working knowledge of the application of IRPCS including:

- Steering & sailing rules (rule 5 – 19)

- Lights & Shapes (rule 20 – 31)

Instructor's signature

7 Maintenance and repair work

- The importance of using protective equipment & safe procedures when carrying out maintenance

- Ability to carry out regular checks on all machinery and equipment as per manufacturer's specification

- How to change fuel & water filters, pump impeller & bleed fuel system on engine

- Understands correct procedures for control, handling and disposal of hazardous substances

- The use & properties of common synthetic rope & can identifying chafe and wear and tear

----
Instructor's signature

8 Victualling

- Understands how to victual with consideration to consumables such as water & gas

Instructor's signature

9 Tender

- Understands loading rules, launch and recovery and can safely operate a tender under power

Instructor's signature

10 Emergency situations

- Understands the correct action to take as watch leader during: fire, sinking or the recovery of a MOB

- Understands how to operate all life saving and firefighting appliances on board including: watertight doors, hatches and storm boards, life rafts, fire extinguishers and distress flares

- Understands helicopter rescue procedure

- Can send a distress message by VHF/DSC

Instructor's signature

11 General watchkeeping

Can carry out watch leading duties while at sea or in harbour with respect to:

- Standing orders & watch bills

- Domestic duties

- The even apportion of work load

- Maintenance of personal standards

Instructor's signature

DAY SKIPPER - TIDAL SYLLABUS

The Day Skipper Course is conducted on board a cruising yacht (7 to 15m LOA), to teach pilotage, navigation, seamanship and boat handling up to the standard required to skipper a small cruising yacht safely by day in tidal waters with which the student is familiar.

1 Preparation for sea
- Is able to prepare a yacht for sea, including engine checks, selection of sails, securing and stowage of all gear on deck and below

Instructor's signature

2 Deck work
- Can reef, shake out reefs and change sails to suit prevailing conditions

- Can prepare an anchor, mooring warps and take charge on deck when mooring alongside, coming to a buoy, anchoring, weighing anchor and slipping from a buoy or an alongside berth

Instructor's signature

3 Navigation
Is proficient in chartwork and routine navigational duties on passage including:

- Taking and plotting visual fixes

- Use of electronic navigation equipment for position fixing

- Use of waypoints

- Working up DR and EP

- Estimating tidal heights and tidal streams

- Working out course to steer to allow for tidal stream, leeway and drift

- Knowledge of IALA buoyage

- Maintenance of navigational records

- Use of echo sounder and lead line

Instructor's signature

4 Pilotage

- Can prepare and execute a pilotage plan for entry into, or departure from, harbour

- Understands the use of leading and clearing lines.

- Use of transits and soundings as aids to pilotage

_____

Instructor's signature

5 Meteorology

- Knows sources of forecast information

- Can interpret shipping forecasts and use a barometer as a forecasting aid

_____

Instructor's signature

6 Rule of the road

- Has a working knowledge of the International Regulations for Preventing Collisions at Sea

_____

Instructor's signature

7 Maintenance and repair work

- Understands and is able to carry out maintenance tasks

- Knows the properties and uses of common synthetic fibre ropes

_____

Instructor's signature

8 Engines

- Knows how to change fuel and water filters, pump impeller and to bleed the fuel system

_____

Instructor's signature

9 Victualling

- Understands how to victual a yacht

_____

Instructor's signature

10 Emergency situations

- Is able to take correct action as skipper for recovery of man overboard

- Understands distress flares and how to use a liferaft

- Can operate a radiotelephone in an emergency and send a distress message

- Understands how to secure a tow

- Understands rescue procedures including helicopter rescue

_____

Instructor's signature

11 Yacht handling under power

- Can bring a boat safely to and from an alongside berth, mooring buoy and anchor under various conditions of wind and tide

_____

12 Yacht handling under sail

- Can bring a boat safely to and from a mooring buoy and anchor under various conditions of wind and tide

- Can steer and trim sails effectively on all points of sailing

_____

13 Passage making

- Can plan and make a coastal passage, taking account of relevant navigational hazards and limitations imposed by the type of boat and the strength of the crew

_____

DAY SKIPPER - NON TIDAL SYLLABUS

The course is conducted on board a cruising yacht (7 to15m LOA), to teach pilotage, navigation, seamanship and boat handling up to the standard required to skipper a small cruising yacht safely by day in non-tidal waters with which the student is familiar.

1 Preparation for sea
- Is able to prepare a yacht for sea, including engine checks, selection of sails, securing and stowage of all gear on deck and below

Instructor's signature

2 Deck work
- Can reef, shake out reefs and change sails to suit prevailing conditions.

- Can prepare an anchor, mooring warps and take charge on deck when mooring alongside, coming to a buoy, anchoring, weighing anchor and slipping from a buoy or an alongside berth, or stern or bow to mooring

Instructor's signature

3 Navigation
- Is proficient in chart-work and routine navigational duties on passage including:

- Taking and plotting visual fixes

- Use of electronic navigation equipment for position fixing

- Use of waypoints

- Working up DR and EP

- Knowledge of IALA buoyage

- Maintenance of navigational records

- Use of echo sounder and lead line

Instructor's signature

4 Pilotage

- Can prepare and execute a pilotage plan for entry into or departure from harbour

- Understands the use of leading and clearing lines

- Use of transits and soundings as aids to pilotage

_____
Instructor's signature

5 Meteorology

- Knows sources of forecast information

- Can interpret forecasts

_____
Instructor's signature

6 Rules of the road

- Has a working knowledge of the International Regulations for Preventing Collisions at Sea

_____
Instructor's signature

7 Maintenance and repair work

- Understands and can carry out maintenance tasks

- Knows the properties and uses of common synthetic fibre ropes

_____
Instructor's signature

8 Engines

- Knows how to change fuel and water filters, pump impeller and to bleed the fuel system

_____
Instructor's signature

9 Victualling

- Understands how to victual a yacht

_____
Instructor's signature

10 Emergency situations

- Is able to take correct action as skipper for recovery of man overboard

- Understands distress flares & how to use a liferaft

- Can operate a radiotelephone in an emergency and send a distress message

- Understands how to secure a tow

- Understands rescue procedures including helicopter rescue

11 Yacht handling under power

- Can bring a boat safely to and from an alongside berth, bow/stern-to mooring, mooring buoy and anchor

12 Yacht handling under sail

- Can bring a boat safely to and from a mooring buoy and anchor

- Can steer and trim sails effectively on all points of sailing

13 Passage making

- Can plan and make a coastal passage, taking account of relevant navigational hazards, local weather patterns and limitations imposed by the type of boat and the strength of the crew

COASTAL SKIPPER - TIDAL SYLLABUS

The aim of the course is to teach the skills and techniques required to skipper a cruising yacht (7-15m LOA) safely on coastal and offshore passages by day and night

1 Passage planning

- Can plan a coastal passage including a consideration of the capability of the yacht, navigation, victualling, weather, ports of refuge, tidal heights and tidal streams, publications required and strategy

- Knows Customs procedures

_____
Instructor's signature

2 Preparation for sea

- Is aware of safety equipment required for offshore passages

- Can prepare a yacht for sea including stowage, safety briefing, watch keeping, delegating responsibilities and equipment and engine checks

_____
Instructor's signature

3 Pilotage

- Can prepare a pilotage plan, with consideration of soundings, transits, clearing bearings, buoyage, port or harbour regulations and tidal considerations

- Can pilot a yacht by day and night

_____
Instructor's signature

4 Passage making and ability as skipper

- Can take charge of a yacht and direct the crew.

- Can organise the navigation, deckwork and domestic duties of a yacht on passage

- Is aware of the significance of meteorological trends

- Is aware of crew welfare on passage

- Can use electronic navigational equipment for planning and undertaking a passage, including the use of waypoints and routes

_____
Instructor's signature

5 Yacht handling under power

- Can contol the yacht effectively in a confined space under power

- All berthing and unberthing situations in various conditions of wind and tide

_____
Instructor's signature

6 Yacht handling under sail

- Can use the sails to control the yacht in a confined space

- Anchoring and mooring in various conditions of wind and tide

- Can sail efficiently on all points of sailing

_____
Instructor's signature

7 Adverse weather conditions

- Preparation for heavy weather and yacht handling in strong winds

- Navigation and general conduct in restricted visibility

_____
Instructor's signature

8 Emergency situations

- Recovery of man overboard under power and sail

- Understands action to be taken when abandoning to the liferaft and during helicopter and lifeboat rescues

_____
Instructor's signature

COASTAL SKIPPER - NON TIDAL SYLLABUS

The aim of this course is to teach the skills and techniques required to skipper a cruising yacht (7-15m LOA) safely on coastal and offshore passages by day and night within any part of the Mediterranean or Baltic Sea.

1 Passage planning

- Can plan a coastal passage including a consideration of the capability of the yacht, navigation, victualling, weather, ports of refuge, publications required and strategy

- Knows Customs procedures

Instructor's signature

2 Preparation for sea

- Is aware of safety equipment required for offshore passages

- Can prepare a yacht for sea including stowage, safety briefing, watch keeping, delegating responsibilities and equipment and engine checks

Instructor's signature

3 Pilotage

- Can prepare a pilotage plan, with consideration of soundings, transits, clearing bearings, buoyage, port or harbour regulations

- Can pilot a yacht by day and night

Instructor's signature

4 Passage making and ability as skipper

- Can take charge of a yacht and direct the crew

- Can organise the navigation, deckwork and domestic duties of a yacht on passage

- Is aware of the significance of meteorological trends

- Is aware of crew welfare on passage

- Can use electronic navigational equipment for planning and undertaking a passage, including the use of waypoints and routes

Instructor's signature

5 Yacht handling under power

- Can control the yacht effectively in a confined space under power

- Can carry out all berthing and unberthing situations

Instructor's signature

6 Yacht handling under sail

- Can use the sails to control the yacht in a confined space

- Can anchor and moor under sail.

- Can sail efficiently on all points of sailing

Instructor's signature

7 Adverse weather conditions

- Preparation for heavy weather and yacht handling in strong winds

- Navigation and general conduct in restricted visibility

Instructor's signature

8 Emergency situations

- Recovery of man overboard under power and sail

- Understands action to be taken when abandoning to the liferaft and during helicopter and lifeboat rescues

Instructor's signature

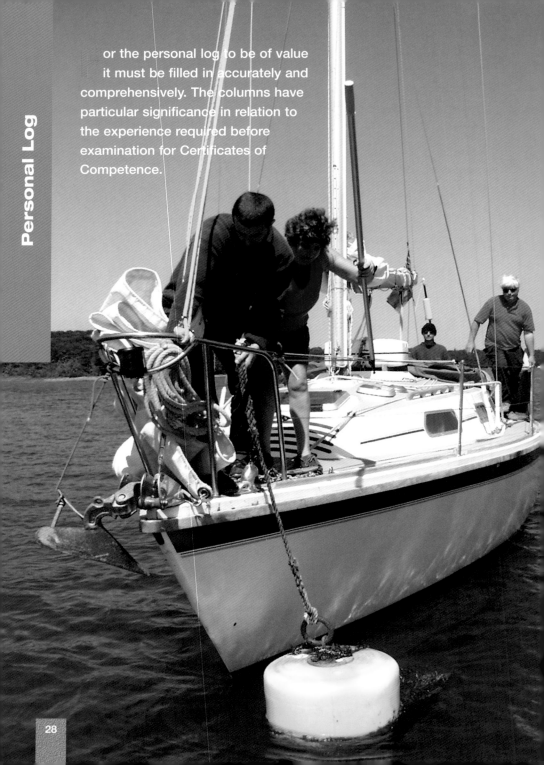

or the personal log to be of value
it must be filled in accurately and
comprehensively. The columns have
particular significance in relation to
the experience required before
examination for Certificates of
Competence.

PERSONAL LOG - CRUISES AND/OR RACES

see page 32

The following notes give guidance on the information to be included and define the terms used.

Column 3 - Details of voyage
It is most important that this includes a record of the capacity in which the cruise was made (eg. crew member, mate of watch, skipper etc.)

Column 4 - Days on board
A day on board is a period of 24 consecutive hours living on board the vessel. Periods of less than 24 hours may not be aggregated to increase the total but a day is not invalidated by leaving the yacht for a few hours during a cruise.

Column 5 - Distance logged
This is the distance sailed by the log, in the open sea, outside natural or artificial harbours in which it would be possible to leave a yacht secured or anchored unattended for a prolonged period.

Tidal
Provided that at least 50% of the qualifying experience for any tidal certificate has been logged in tidal seas, the balance may be made up of experience in non-tidal seas.

Column 6 - Night hours
This is hours on watch or taking an active part in the navigation or handling of the yacht, at sea between sunset and sunrise.

Column 7 - Signature of skipper
Holders of logbooks may sign for cruises during which they were skipper of the yacht.

Retrospective logging of experience
Page 31 includes a section for candidates to record, in general terms, experience gained prior to acquiring the logbook. The experience requirements for examinations for Yachtmaster Offshore and Coastal Skipper must have been gained within 10 years of the examination.

RYA/MCA Yachtmaster Examinations

Record of qualifying passages
Full details of the qualifying passages required for the Yachtmaster Offshore examination should be recorded on page 53.

Quality of experience
The requirements for experience prior to examination for RYA/MCA certificates can only be defined in quantitative terms. However, the quality of experience is just as important and although it would be impossible to lay down absolute requirements without producing an unduly complicated and restrictive set of rules, the attention of all candidates is drawn to the following notes.

Geographical breadth of experience

It is relatively simple to visit harbours and anchorages with which one is familiar and has local knowledge. However, a competent yachtsman should be able to enter any harbour in which there is sufficient depth, given an adequate chart and sailing directions. The skill of interpreting published information on unfamiliar harbours is best acquired by practice and every opportunity should be taken to visit small harbours and anchorages. Entering harbour by night calls for an acquired skill in identifying navigational lights or picking out unlit marks against the background of the shore lights. Again, practice is the key to success.

Boat handling under sail

Now that so many harbours are crowded with permanent moorings, there is little scope in the normal course of cruising to practise the traditional skills of handling a yacht under sail in confined waters. However, these skills are important so that in the event of a broken-down engine or a fouled propeller the yacht is not totally disabled. Practice in handling a yacht under sail, approaching and leaving a mooring or anchor, recovering a man overboard and sailing in narrow channels are all essential in order to ensure that the skipper and crew can, if necessary, carry out manoeuvres without recourse to an auxiliary.

Adverse weather conditions

Skippers are most thoroughly tested when they have to cope with gale force winds or fog at sea. It is possible, by sailing within strict self-imposed limits and never making passages which place the yacht more than a few hours from a safe harbour, to avoid adverse weather conditions but to do so invariably limits experience. It is not recommended that anyone should go to sea under adverse conditions for the sole purpose of experiencing a gale or fog but neither should candidates for RYA/MCA certificates adopt an over-cautious approach.

Long passages

In many parts of the world, particularly in popular yachting centres, it is possible to cruise over a wide area without ever making a passage longer than 18-24 hours. Such passages can be accomplished without the need for an effective watch-keeping system and tend to encourage day-sailing rather than passage-making. Candidates should endeavour to gain experience of longer passages of two or three days or more, to ensure that they understand how a yacht and crew must be organised during a prolonged period at sea.

Racing

The ability to sail a yacht efficiently in terms of helmsmanship and sail setting and trimming is a skill which candidates for RYA/MCA examinations are encouraged to acquire. The best way to measure and to improve these skills is by taking part in races. There are also skills such as the ability to sail so that the yacht places the minimum demands on her gear and on the strength and stamina of her crew which are the antithesis of those required when racing. The candidate whose normal pattern of sailing is heavily racing-based may need to experience short-handed passage-making to develop these skills.

Dinghy sailing

Many sailors believe that a dinghy is the best type of boat in which to learn to sail. A light, unballasted sailing dinghy is certainly likely to be less forgiving of bad helmsmanship or crewing than is a heavy displacement cruising yacht. There is no arrangement in the syllabus for dinghy sailing to be substituted for cruising experience as part of the necessary seatime. However, anyone who is setting out to learn to sail should certainly consider taking a dinghy sailing course, even though his ultimate aim may be to sail exclusively in larger craft.

Summary of experience prior to record in personal log

Year	Broad details of experience [1]	Days on board	Distance logged	Night hours	Skipper's signature [2]
		Estimated	Estimated		

1 include boats sailed, sailing area and capacity in which sailed
2 if available

Personal log of cruises and/or races

1. Dates From To	2. Name of vessel Class, size inc LOA or tonnage	3. Details of voyage max wind force, ports visited, capacity in which sailing	4. Days on board	5. Distance logged tidal/non-tidal	6. Night hours	7. Skipper's signature
Specimen entry 19–27th Sept 2004	WAVERIDER Farr 38	Port Bishop – Bridgetown – Fairlie – Braydon Is. – Port Bishop	8	145 Tidal	7	Wynne Chandle
6th–13th APRIL 2007	"BONCHO" BAVARIA 36 38ft 10a	MARINA SAN MIGUEL – LOS GIGANTS – SAN SABASTIAN – SANTAGO – SAN SABASTIAN – LOS CRISTIANOS EL PRIS – CHARLANA SAN MIGUEL MAY F8	7	136 TIDAL	3	Club Sail Sea School MASTER EST. 1986

Totals carried forward

Personal log of cruises and/or races

1. Dates From To	2. Name of vessel Class, size inc LOA or tonnage	3. Details of voyage max wind force, ports visited, capacity in which sailing	4. Days on board	5. Distance logged tidal/non-tidal	6. Night hours	7. Skipper's signature

Personal log of cruises and/or races

1. Dates From To	2. Name of vessel Class, size inc LOA or tonnage	3. Details of voyage max wind force, ports visited, capacity in which sailing	4. Days on board	5. Distance logged tidal/non-tidal	6. Night hours	7. Skipper's signature

Personal log of cruises and/or races

Totals brought forward

Totals carried forward

1. Dates From To	2. Name of vessel Class, size inc LOA or tonnage	3. Details of voyage max wind force, ports visited, capacity in which sailing	4. Days on board	5. Distance logged tidal/non-tidal	6. Night hours	7. Skipper's signature

35

Personal log of cruises and/or races

1. Dates From To	2. Name of vessel Class, size inc LOA or tonnage	3. Details of voyage max wind force, ports visited, capacity in which sailing	4. Days on board	5. Distance logged tidal/non-tidal	6. Night hours	7. Skipper's signature

Personal log of cruises and/or races

1. Dates From To	2. Name of vessel Class, size inc LOA or tonnage	3. Details of voyage max wind force, ports visited, capacity in which sailing	4. Days on board	5. Distance logged tidal/non-tidal	6. Night hours	7. Skipper's signature

37

Personal log of cruises and/or races

1. Dates From To	2. Name of vessel Class, size inc LOA or tonnage	3. Details of voyage max wind force, ports visited, capacity in which sailing	4. Days on board	5. Distance logged tidal/non-tidal	6. Night hours	7. Skipper's signature

Personal log of cruises and/or races

1. Dates From To	2. Name of vessel Class, size inc LOA or tonnage	3. Details of voyage max wind force, ports visited, capacity in which sailing	4. Days on board	5. Distance logged tidal/non-tidal	6. Night hours	7. Skipper's signature

Personal log of cruises and/or races

1. Dates From To	2. Name of vessel Class, size inc LOA or tonnage	3. Details of voyage max wind force, ports visited, capacity in which sailing	4. Days on board	5. Distance logged tidal/non-tidal	6. Night hours	7. Skipper's signature

Personal log of cruises and/or races

Totals brought forward

Totals carried forward

1. Dates From To	2. Name of vessel Class, size inc LOA or tonnage	3. Details of voyage max wind force, ports visited, capacity in which sailing	4. Days on board	5. Distance logged tidal/non-tidal	6. Night hours	7. Skipper's signature

Personal log of cruises and/or races

Totals brought forward

Totals carried forward

1. Dates From To	2. Name of vessel Class, size inc LOA or tonnage	3. Details of voyage max wind force, ports visited, capacity in which sailing	4. Days on board	5. Distance logged tidal/non-tidal	6. Night hours	7. Skipper's signature

42

Summary of personal log

	Day	Distance logged	Night hours
TOTALS FOR 20..			
TOTALS FOR 20..			
TOTALS FOR 20..			
TOTALS FOR 20..			
TOTALS FOR 20..			
TOTALS FOR 20..			
TOTALS FOR 20..			
TOTALS FOR 20..			
TOTALS FOR 20..			
TOTALS FOR 20..			
TOTALS			

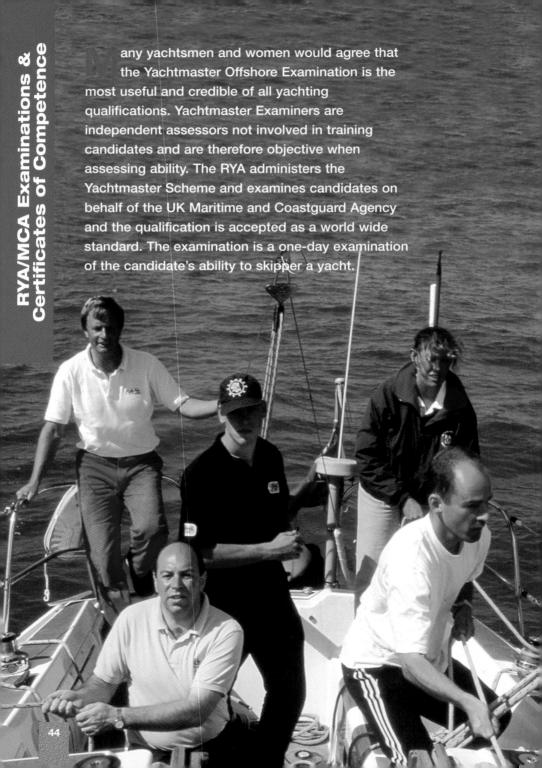

any yachtsmen and women would agree that the Yachtmaster Offshore Examination is the most useful and credible of all yachting qualifications. Yachtmaster Examiners are independent assessors not involved in training candidates and are therefore objective when assessing ability. The RYA administers the Yachtmaster Scheme and examines candidates on behalf of the UK Maritime and Coastguard Agency and the qualification is accepted as a world wide standard. The examination is a one-day examination of the candidate's ability to skipper a yacht.

EXAMINATIONS FOR RYA/MCA
CERTIFICATES OF COMPETENCE

RYA/MCA Coastal Skipper, Yachtmaster Offshore and Yachtmaster Ocean Certificates of Competence are gained by examination, conducted by RYA Yachtmaster Examiners who are independent of sailing schools. The previous experience required before taking these examinations, and the scope of the syllabus, is shown on the following pages. There is no requirement to attend a sailing school course before taking an examination, although many

candidates have found it helpful to brush up their skills at a school. Skippers should ensure that they are familiar with the handling and other characteristics of any vessel they take to sea.

Certificate of Competence are not required on board British flag pleasure vessels of less than 24 metres load line length or less than 80gross tonns.

Megayacht qualifications

UK commercial pleasure vessels of more than 24 metres load line length are subject to the Training and Certification Guidance Part 21 of MGN 195(M).

Full details are given on the website www.megayachtcode.com.

RYA/MCA Certificates of Competence with a commercial endorsement can be used for vessels up to 200GT and as an entry into these qualifications.

Vessels under 24m in length used for sport or recreation on a commercial basis

Vessels used for sport or recreation on a commercial basis are subject to Merchant Shipping legislation. The use of Coastal Skipper, Yachtmaster Offshore and Yachtmaster Ocean certificates is permitted for the skippers of these vessels, provided that the certificates are endorsed 'Valid for pleasure vessels up to 24m in length used for commercial purposes'.

To obtain this endorsement an applicant must obtain a Medical Fitness Certificate and attend a Basic Sea Survival Course.

Medical fitness forms and details of Basic Sea Survival Courses are available from the RYA or www.rya.org.uk.

The endorsement for commercial use is valid for five years. It may be renewed by providing evidence of continuing satisfactory service at sea as skipper or mate of a small commercial vessel and a Medical Fitness Certificate.

Withdrawal of Certificates

The Yachtmaster Qualification Panel reserves the right to withdraw certificates at any time if due cause is shown.

Own boat exams

For the practical examination for Coastal Skipper and Yachtmaster Offshore, candidates must provide a cruising yacht, normally not less than 7 metres LOA, in sound, seaworthy condition and equipped to the standard set out in the RYA book *Cruising Yacht Safety (C8)*. The yacht must be equipped with a full and up-to-date set of charts and navigational publications and be efficiently crewed, as the examiner will not take part in the management of the yacht during the examination.

Booking an examination

You can book an exam at www.rya.org.uk or contact:

Southern
Royal Yachting Association
RYA House
Ensign Way
Hamble Southampton
Hampshire SO31 4YA
Tel: 0845 345 0400

East Anglia
West Mersea Yacht Club
116 Coast Road
West Mersea
Colchester CO5 8PB
Tel: 01206 383306

Wales
RYA Examination Centre
16 Friars Road
Barry Island
Glamorgan CF62 8TR
Tel: 01446 734836

Scotland
RYA Scotland
Caledonia House
South Gyle
Edinburgh EH12 9DQ
Tel: 0131 317 7388

Examinations for service personnel are also conducted by the JSASTC, RNSA, RAFSA, and ASA. Servicemen should consult the JSASTC or their Sailing Association for details of examination arrangements.

Exams through a training centre

If you take a course at an RYA Training Centre the exam can be arranged through the centre.

Exams outside the UK

Overseas examinations must be organised through an RYA Training Centre recognised for practical cruising courses. The school must notify the RYA of any overseas examinations and the location must be approved by the RYA.

Exams in New Zealand are organised through CBES

Coastguard Boating Education Service
2 Fred Thomas drive
Takapuna
Auckland
New Zealand
jan@cbes.org.nz

Coastal Skipper Certificate of Competence

The Coastal Skipper has the knowledge needed to skipper a yacht on coastal cruises but does not necessarily have the experience needed to undertake longer passages.

Exam duration

The exam will take about 6 to 10 hours for one candidate and 8 to 14 hours for two. Candidates will be set tasks to demonstrate their ability as a Coastal Skipper and may also be asked questions on any part of the syllabus for all practical and shorebased courses up to Coastal Skipper

---

Pre-exam requirement

To take the practical examination, candidates must be aged 17 or over and require:

Radio Operator's Qualification - A Restricted (VHF only) Radio Operator's Certificate or a GMDSS Short Range Certificate or higher grade of marine radio certificate.

First Aid - A valid First Aid Certificate. First Aid qualifications held by Police, Fire and Armed Services are also acceptable.

Seatime - 800 miles logged within 10 years prior to examination, 30 days living on board, 2 days as skipper and 12 night hours.

For holders of the Coastal Skipper Practical Course Completion Certificate, the seatime requirement is reduced to: 400 miles, 20 days living on board, 12 night hours, 2 days as skipper. Half the qualifying seatime must have been conducted in tidal waters.

Yachtmaster Offshore Certificate of Competence

The Yachtmaster Offshore is competent to skipper a cruising yacht on any passage during which the yacht is no more than 150 miles from harbour.

Exam duration

The yachtmaster exam will take about 8 to12 hours for one candidate and 10 to18 hours for two. Candidates will be set tasks to demonstrate their ability as skipper of an offshore cruising yacht and may also be asked questions on any part of the syllabus for all courses except Yachtmaster Ocean.

Pre-exam requirement

To take the practical examination, candidates must be aged 18 or over and require:

Radio Operator's Qualification - A Restricted (VHF only) Radio Operator's Certificate or a GMDSS Short Range Certificate or higher grade of marine radio certificate.

First Aid - A valid First Aid Certificate. First Aid qualifications held by Police, Fire and Armed Services are also acceptable.

Seatime - 50 days, 2,500 miles, including at least 5 passages over 60 miles measured along the rhumb line from the port of departure to the destination, acting as skipper for at least two of these passages and including two which have involved overnight passages. 5 days experience as skipper. Half the qualifying seatime must have been conducted in tidal waters.

Conversion Practical Examinations

Holders of the Yachtmaster Offshore Sail Certificate may take a conversion examination to obtain the Yachtmaster Offshore Power Certificate. Yachtmaster Offshore Power candidates may convert to sail. The same rules apply but the exam may be slightly longer.

The exam fee set by the RYA is approximately half that of a full examination.

Exam duration

The exam will take about three hours. The examiner may ask questions or set tasks on any part of the syllabus but will concentrate on those sections which are markedly different in a motor cruiser e.g. boat handling, passage planning, radar.

Pre-exam requirement

At least half the required experience for Yachtmaster must be in a power vessel such as a motor cruiser i.e: 1250 miles • 25 days • 3 days as skipper • 3 passages over 60 miles including, 1 overnight and 1 as skipper.

Yachtmaster Ocean Certificate of Competence

The Yachtmaster Ocean is experienced and competent to skipper a yacht on passages of any length in all parts of the world.

Form of examination

The exam consists of an oral and a written test.

Oral

The candidate must provide the examiner with:

a) A narrative account of the planning and execution of the qualifying passage.

b) Navigational records, completed on board a yacht on passage, out of sight of land, showing that the candidate has navigated the yacht without the use of electronic navigational aids. The records must include as a minimum: planning, reduction and plotting of a sun-run-meridian altitude sight and a compass check carried out using the bearing of the sun, moon, a star or a planet.

During the oral test the candidate may be required to answer questions on all aspects of ocean passage making in a yacht, including passage planning, navigation, worldwide meteorology, crew management and yacht preparation, maintenance and repairs.

Written

The written exam will include questions on sights and sight reduction and worldwide meteorology.

Candidates who hold the Certificate of Satisfactory Completion of the RYA/MCA Yachtmaster Ocean Shorebased Course, a Royal Navy Ocean Navigation Certificate or a MCA Certificate of Competence as a Deck Officer will be exempt from the written examination.

Pre-exam requirement

All candidates must:

(i) Hold an RYA/MCA Yachtmaster Offshore Certificate of Competence. An RYA/MCA Coastal Skipper Certificate does not qualify.

(ii) Have completed, as skipper or mate of a yacht, a qualifying passage which meets the following criteria:

a) The candidate was fully involved in the planning of the passage, including selection of the route, the navigational plan, checking the material condition of the yacht and her equipment, storing with spare gear, water and victuals and organising the watch-keeping routine.

b) During the passage a minimum non-stop distance of 600 miles must have been run by the log, the yacht must have been at sea continuously for at least 96 hours and the yacht must have been more than 50 miles from land while sailing a distance of at least 200 miles.

(iii) Hold a First Aid qualification, as for Yachtmaster Offshore.

COASTAL SKIPPER AND YACHTMASTER OFFSHORE EXAM SYLLABUS

Candidates may be given the opportunity to demonstrate knowledge or competence in the areas listed below. In each section the examiner will expect to see the candidate take full responsibility for the management of the yacht and crew.

In Yachtmaster Offshore exams the candidate will be expected to demonstrate competence based on broad experience.

In Coastal Skipper exams the candidate will be expected to demonstrate understanding but may not have had the opportunity to practise all aspects of the syllabus under a range of different weather conditions.

1 International Regulations for preventing Collisions at Sea

Questions will be confined to the International Regulations and although candidates must be aware of the existence of Local Regulations, they will not be expected to memorise specific local regulations.

- General rules (1-3)
- Steering and sailing rules (4-19)
- Lights and shapes (20-31)
- Sound and light signals (32-37)
- Signals for vessels fishing in close proximity (Annex II)
- Distress signals (Annex IV)

2 Safety

Candidates will be expected to know what safety equipment should be carried on board a yacht, based either on the recommendations in the RYA Boat Safety Handbook (C8), the ISAF Special Regulations or the Codes of Practice for the Safety of Small Commercial Vessels. In particular, candidates must know the responsibilities of a skipper in relation to:

- Safety harnesses
- Lifejackets
- Distress flares
- Fire prevention and fighting

- Liferafts
- Knowledge of rescue procedures.
- Helicopter rescue

3 Boat Handling

Candidates for Coastal Skipper examinations will be expected to answer questions or demonstrate ability in simple situations only. Candidates for Yachtmaster Offshore will be expected to answer questions or demonstrate ability in more complex situations and will also be expected to show a higher level of expertise:

- Coming to and weighing anchor under power or sail in various conditions of wind and tide
- All berthing and unberthing situations in various conditions of wind and tide
- Recovery of man overboard
- Towing under open sea conditions and in confined areas
- Boat handling in confined areas under sail
- Boat handling in heavy weather
- Helmsmanship and sail trim to sail to best advantage
- Use of warps for securing in an alongside berth and for shifting berth or winding

4 General seamanship, including maintenance

- Properties, use and care of synthetic fibre ropes
- Knots
- General deck-work at sea and in harbour
- Engine operations and routine checks
- Improvisation of jury rigs following gear failure

5 Responsibilities of skipper

- Can skipper a yacht and manage the crew
- Communication with crew
- Delegation of responsibility and watch-keeping organisation
- Preparing yacht for sea and for adverse weather
- Tactics for heavy weather and restricted visibility
- Emergency and distress situations
- Victualling for a cruise and feeding at sea
- Customs procedures
- Standards of behaviour and courtesy

6 Navigation

- Charts, navigational publications and sources of navigational information
- Chartwork including position fixing and shaping course to allow for tidal stream and leeway
- Tide and tidal stream calculations
- Buoyage and visual aids to navigation
- Instruments including compasses, logs, echo sounders, radio navaids and chartwork instruments
- Passage planning and navigational tactics
- Pilotage techniques
- Navigational records
- Limits of navigational accuracy and margins of safety
- Lee shore dangers
- Use of electronic navigation aids for passage planning and passage navigation
- Use of waypoints and electronic routeing

7 Meteorology

- Definition of terms
- Sources of weather forecasts
- Weather systems and local weather effects
- Interpretation of weather forecasts, barometric trends and visible phenomena
- Ability to make passage planning decisions based on forecast information

8 Signals

- Candidates for Yachtmaster Offshore and Coastal Skipper must hold the Restricted (VHF only) Certificate of Competence in radiotelephony or a higher grade of certificate in radiotelephony.

RYA/MCA offshore qualifying passages

Port of departure time date	Destination time date	Distance	Sailing capacity	Skipper's signature
Summer Bay 2000 24.09.04	*Port Erinsborough* 1450 25.09.04	*82M*	*Skipper*	*C Heyes*

Specimen entry

RYA/MCA Yachtmaster Ocean passage

Passage completed on board yacht ....

Type of yacht, inc LOA ....

Port of departure ....Time/Date ....

Port of arrival ....Time/Date ....

Over 50M from land between position ....Time/Date ....

and position ....Time/Date ....

a total of .... hours, for a distance of .... miles

Sailing as Skipper/Mate of Watch (delete as appropriate) throughout the passage.

Total distance sailed .... M

Signature of Skipper ....

The shorebased courses are designed to complement courses in the various RYA Practical schemes. The longer courses (40 hours) are typically run over two terms of evening classes or five days of intensive tuition, although many schools offer variations, including distance learnng. Taking a one-day course will enable you to extend your knowledge and skills in a specialist area and some courses, such as the VHF Short Range Certificate, are a pre-requisite for higher qualifications such as the RYA Yachtmaster Certificate of Competence.

Course Completion Certificates

The authority to award certificates of satisfactory completion of shorebased courses is delegated to RYA Training Centres, which may be Local Education Authority evening classes, clubs, sailing schools or correspondence schools.

All instructors must hold an RYA/MCA Yachtmaster Offshore Certificate of Competence and be an active cruising or offshore racing skipper. All potential shorebased instructors will be asked to attend an RYA Shorebased Instructor's, training and familiarisation weekend.

The school must provide a suitable classroom where all the students can undertake chartwork simultaneously.

Certificates of satisfactory completion of courses are, as the name implies, awarded only following completion of a course. The theory or written exams may not be taken as a separate entity. However, anyone who has the necessary qualifying experience may take the full practical examination for Coastal Skipper or Yachtmaster Offshore (see pages 16 thro' 27).

Assessment during shorebased courses

A standard set of assessment papers for each course is provided. While many of these papers are used informally, some are worked under invigilation to provide an objective test of ability at the end of the course.

Layout of syllabi

An indication of the minimum recommended teaching time for each subject is given in each syllabus. The total time for each syllabus is approximately 40 hours.

The courses also include assessment papers which involve an additional 14 hours work. Sufficient time should be allowed for completion of these exercises and subsequent discussion of them, together with additional exercises set by instructors and revision which may add anything up to 100% to the minimum recommended teaching times. An indication of the depth of knowledge required is also given, the following abbreviations being used:

A Full knowledge **B** Working knowledge **C** Outline knowledge

International Regulations for Preventing Collisions at Sea

Students are required to have a full knowledge of the regulations before completion of the shorebased course for Coastal Skipper and Yachtmaster Offshore. There is, however, insufficient time available in the course to teach the subject fully. The RYA book *International Regulations for Preventing Collisions at Sea (G2)* or *A Seaman's Guide to the Rule of the Road* are useful books for study of the regulations.

Feedback

The student's assessment pack includes two forms requesting feedback about the courses. Please help the RYA to improve the courses by returning one to the school and the other to the RYA.

DAY SKIPPER SYLLABUS

A comprehensive introduction to chart work, navigation, meteorology and the basics of seamanship for Competent Crew. You will find this course invaluable if you want to learn how to start making decisions on board.

	Minimum time (hours)	Depth of knowledge
1. Nautical terms	2	
• Parts of a boat and hull		B
• General nautical terminology		B
2 Ropework	1	
• Knowledge of the properties of synthetic ropes in common use		B
3 Anchorwork		1
• Characteristics of different types of anchor		B
• Considerations to be taken into account when anchoring		B
4 Safety	3	
• Knowledge of the safety equipment to be carried, it's stowage and use (see RYA Boat Safety Handbook, C8)		B
• Fire precautions and fire fighting		B
• Use of personal safety equipment, harnesses and lifejackets		B
• Ability to send a distress signal by VHF radiotelephone		B
• Basic knowledge of rescue procedures including helicopter rescue		B
5 International regulations for preventing collisions at sea	3	
• Steering and sailing rules (5, 7, 8, 9, 10 and 12-19)		A
• General rules (all other rules)		B

	Minimum time (hours)	Depth of knowledge

6 Definition of position, course and speed — 1
- Latitude and longitude — B
- Knowledge of standard navigational terms — B
- True bearings and courses — B
- The knot — C

7 Navigational charts and publications — 2
- Information shown on charts, chart symbols and representation of direction and distance — B
- Navigational publications in common use — C
- Chart correction — C

8 Navigational drawing instruments — 1
- Use of parallel rulers, dividers and proprietary plotting instruments — B

9 Compass — 2
- Application of variation — B
- Awareness of deviation and its causes — C
- Use of hand-bearing compass — B

10 Chartwork — 6
- Dead reckoning and estimated position including an awareness of leeway — B / C
- Techniques of visual fixing — B
- Satellite-derived positions — B
- Use of waypoints to fix position — A
- Course to steer — B

11 Tides and tidal streams — 4
- Tidal definitions, levels and datum — B
- Tide tables — B
- Use of Admiralty method of determining tidal height at standard port and awareness of corrections for secondary ports — B
- Use of tidal diamonds and tidal stream atlases for chartwork — B

	Minimum time (hours)	Depth of knowledge

12 Visual aids to navigation
	1	
• Lighthouses and beacons, light characteristics		B

13 Meteorology
	3	
• Sources of broadcast meteorological information		B
• Knowledge of terms used in shipping forecasts, including the Beaufort scale, and their significance to small craft		B
• Basic knowledge of highs, lows and fronts		C

14 Passage planning
	4	
• Preparation of navigational plan for short coastal passages		C
• Meteorological considerations in planning short coastal passages		C
• Use of waypoints on passage		B
• Importance of confirmation of position by an independent source		A
• Keeping a navigational record		A

15 Navigation in restricted visibility
	1	
• Precautions to be taken in, and limitations imposed by, fog		B

16 Pilotage
	4	
• Use of transits, leading lines and clearing lines		B
• IALA system of buoyage for Region A		B
• Use of sailing directions		B
• Pilotage plans and harbour entry		B

17 Marine environment
	1	
• Responsibility for avoiding pollution and protecting the marine environment		B

COASTAL SKIPPER AND YACHTMASTER SYLLABUS

This is an advanced course in navigation and meteorology for candidates for the Coastal Skipper and Yachtmaster Offshore Certificate. The syllabus makes some provision for the revision of subjects in the Day Skipper Course but those who have not acquired the knowledge set out in the Day Skipper Course are unlikely to be able to assimilate all the subjects covered in this advanced course in the time available.

The assumed level of knowledge before starting this course is the Day Skipper Shorebased Course.

	Minimum time (hours)	Depth of knowledge
1 Position	6	
• Dead reckoning and estimated position		B
• Satellite-derived position		A
• Use of waypoints to fix position		A
• Radar fixes		B
• Techniques of visual fixing		B
• Fixes using a mixture of position lines		B
• Relative accuracy of different methods of position fixing		A
• Areas of uncertainty		C
2 The magnetic compass	2	
• Allowance for variation		B
• Change of variation with time and position		B
• Causes of deviation		B
• Swing for deviation (but not correction)		C
• Allowance for deviation		C
• Different types of compass		C

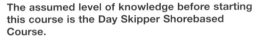

	Minimum time (hours)	Depth of knowledge
3 Tides	4	
• Causes of tides - Springs and Neaps		C
• Tide tables - sources		C
• Tidal levels and datum		B
• Standard and secondary ports		B
• Tidal anomalies (Solent, etc.)		C
4 Tidal streams	3	
• Sources of tidal information		B
• Tidal stream information in sailing directions and Yachtsmen's Almanacs		B
• Allowance for tidal streams in computing a course to steer		A
• Tide rips, overfalls and races		B
• Tidal observation buoys, beacons etc.		B
5 Buoyage	1	
• IALA system buoyage in Region A		B
• Limitations of buoys as navigational aids		C
6 Lights	1	
• Characteristics		B
• Ranges – visual, luminous and nominal		C
• Rising and dipping distances		C
• Light lists		C
7 Pilotage	3	
• Harbour regulations and control signals		A
• Methods of pre-planning		B
• Clearing lines		A
• Use of soundings		B
• Transits and leading lines		B

	Minimum time (hours)	Depth of knowledge
8 GPS and chart plotters	3	
• Principles of operation and limitations of use		A
• Raster and vector charts		C
• Datum		C
• Importance of confirmation of position by an independent source and keeping a separate record of position		A
• Importance of paper charts		B
9 Echo sounders	1/2	
• Principles of operation and limitations of use		C
10 Logs (speed and distance measuring)	1/2	
• Principles of operation and limitations of use		C
11 Deck log	1/2	
• Importance of log as yacht's official document		B
• Layout of log, hourly and occasional entries		B
12 Meteorology	6	
• Basic terms, the Beaufort scale		B
• Air masses		B
• Cloud types		B
• Weather patterns associated with pressure and frontal systems		B
• Sources of weather forecasts		B
• Ability to interpret a shipping forecast, weatherfax and weather satellite information		B
• Land and sea breezes		B
• Sea fog		C
• Use of a barometer as a forecasting aid		B
13 Rule of the Road	1	
• A sound knowledge of the International Regulations for Preventing Collisions at Sea, except Annexes 1 and 3		A

	Minimum time (hours)	Depth of knowledge
14 Safety at Sea	2	
• Personal safety, use of lifejackets, safety harnesses and lifelines		B
• Fire prevention and fire fighting		B
• Distress signals		B
• Coastguard and Boat Safety Scheme		C
• Preparation for heavy weather		B
• Liferafts and helicopter rescue		B
• Understanding of capabilities of vessel and basic knowledge of stability		C
15 Navigation in restricted visibility	1	
• Precautions to be taken in fog		B
• Limitations to safe navigation imposed by fog		B
• Navigation strategy in poor visibility		B
16 Passage planning	5	
• Preparation of charts and notebook for route planning and making, and use at sea		B
• Customs regulations as they apply to yachts		C
• Routine for navigating in coastal waters		B
• Strategy for course laying		B
• Use of waypoints and routes		A
• Use of weather forecast information for passage planning strategy		B
• Sources of local and national regulations		B
17 Marine Environment	1/2	
• Responsibility to minimise pollution and protect the marine environment		B

YACHTMASTER OCEAN SYLLABUS

This is a course in astro-navigation and worldwide meteorology which also reveals the mysteries of the sextant. It assumes a knowledge of all subjects covered in the other shorebased courses

Minimum
time (hours)

1 The earth and the celestial sphere

2

- Definition of observer's zenith and position of a heavenly body in terms of latitude, longitude, GHA and declination

- Right angle relationships, latitude and co-lat, declination and polar distance

- Relationship between GHA, longitude and LHA

- Tabulation of declination in nautical almanac

- Rate of increase of hour angle with time

2 The PZX triangle

3

- The tabulated components of the triangle, LHA, co-lat and polar distance

- The calculable components, zenith distance and azimuth

- Relationship between zenith distance and altitude

- Introduction to the tabular method of solution in the Air Navigation Tables and the basic sight form

- The use of calculators for the solution of the PZX triangle

3 The sextant

2

- Practical guide to the use and care of a sextant at sea

- Conversion of sextant altitude to true altitude

- Application of dip, index error and refraction

- Correction of side error, perpendicularity, index error and collimation error

4 Measurement of time
- Definition of, and relationship between, UT, LMT, standard time and zone time
- Rating of chronometers and watches

5 Meridian altitudes
- Forecasting time of meridian altitude
- Reduction of meridian altitude sights

6 Sun, star and other sights
- Reduction and plotting of sun sights using Air
- Navigation Tables
- Awareness of use of calculator for sight reduction
- The plotting of a sun-run-sun meridian altitude
- Awareness of the reduction and plotting of sights obtained from stars, moon and planets

7 Compass checking
- Use of amplitude and azimuth tables systems and/or calculator

8 Satellite Navigation Systems
- Principles and limitations of use of all systems

9 Great circle sailing
- Comparison of rhumb lines and great circles
- Vertices and composite tracks
- The computation of a series of rhumb lines approximating to a great circle by use of gnomonic and Mercator projections

10 Meteorology
- General pressure distribution and prevailing winds over the oceans of the world
- Tropical revolving storms, seasonal occurrence and forecasting by observation

11 *Passage planning*
- Publications available to assist with planning of long passages (routeing charts, ocean passages of the world and other publications)

- Preparation for ocean passage including survival equipment, victualling, water and fuel management, chafe protection, spares and maintenance

12 *Passage making*
3
- Navigational routine
- Watchkeeping
- Crew management

13 *Communications*
2
- Satellite and terrestrial systems
- Weather information

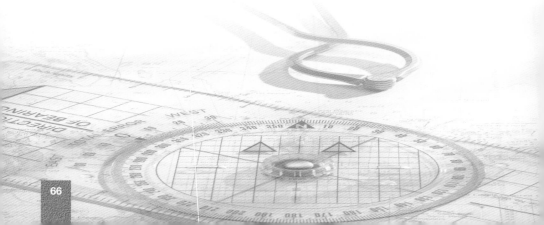

The RYA offers a range of one day courses which complement the practical and navigation courses. Some are essential for those who wish to take their Yachtmaster and Coastal Skipper certificates of Competence or work commercially as a skipper.

First Aid Course

VHF Course

Radar Course

Diesel Engine Course

Sea Survival Course

FIRST AID

In a medical emergency a little first aid knowledge and immediate action can save lives, especially in remote locations. This one day course is designed to provide a working knowledge of first aid for people using small craft and to support skippers of yacht and motor vessels. It fulfils the requirements for skippers of small craft working within 60 miles of a safe haven. The course is MCA and HSE approved.

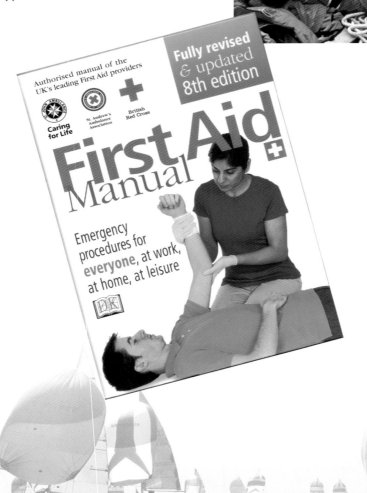

RESTRICTED (VHF ONLY) RADIO OPERATOR

If you own a marine radio hand held or fixed set, you are required by law to hold an operators licence - learn the procedures for operation and gain the qualification on this one day course.

VHF G22/02

VHF radio
(inc GMDSS)

VHF G26/02

VHF Radio
Short Range Certificate
Syllabus & Sample
Exam Questions

RYA

DIESEL ENGINE

This one day course provides an awareness of the main systems of a marine diesel engine and teaches the ability to take simple measures to prevent mechanical breakdown at sea and rectify defects which do not require workshop support. Mechnical failure is the main course of lifeboat callout to yachts and motor cruisers. Basic maintenance and engine care may make sure you are not part of these figures.

Course duration

The minimum duration of the course is six hours.

A marine diesel engine (not necessarily in working condition) will be provided for practical sessions. (No more than six students to one engine.) Instructors will have attended an RYA training course.

Pre-course knowledge

Nil

1 Introduction
- Principles of the diesel engine

2 The four-stroke cycle
- Naturally aspirated engines
- Turbocharging
- Intercooling/aftercooling

3 The fuel system
- The basic system
- The tank
- The water-separating pre-filter

BASIC SEA SURVIVAL FOR SMALL CRAFT

It is a well proven fact that in the event of an emergency at sea, people who have received training are more likely to survive.

This course covers preparation for survival, lifejackets, search and rescue and a practical session in a swimming pool with a liferaft.

Course duration

The course duration is one day, including a two hour practical session with a liferaft in the water.

Pre-course knowledge

Nil

1 Preparation for sea survival

- Survival difficulties
- Survival requirements
- Equipment available
- Actions prior to abandonment

2 Lifejackets and liferafts

- Lifejacket design and construction correct donning procedure, purpose and use of lifejackets
- Safety harness - purpose and use

- Liferafts -

    stowage and containment on board -

    types, design and construction

    launching

    abandoning the vessel and boarding liferaft -

    righting a capsized liferaft -

    liferaft equipment -

    initial actions to be taken in a liferaft

3 Principles of survival
- Methods to increase chances of survival
- Signs, symptoms and treatment of hypothermia
- Symptoms, method of treatment for sunburn, heat exhaustion and heatstroke
- Survival routines to aid location
- Correct use of pyrotechnics and other location aids
- Water rationing - procedures
- Dehydration and preventative measures
- Food rationing
- Sources of food

4 Survival craft ailments

5 Raft management

6 Search and rescue
- Rescue by helicopter or vessel
- Role of HM Coastguard
- UK and International SAR Organisation
- Other services

RADAR

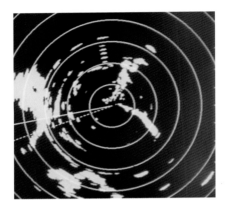

The aim of the course is to teach students to use small boat Radar to assist decision-making in navigation, pilotage and collision avoidance.

The course can be conducted ashore using RYA approved software, or afloat on an authorized vessel. The maximum number of students per course will be four afloat or three per screen when conducted ashore. The instructor will have attended an RYA training course.

Course duration
The minimum duration of the course is one day.

Pre-course knowledge
Nil

1   Switching on and setting up
* Adjusting brilliance, contrast, gain, range and tuning

2   Refining the picture:
* Adjust the sea clutter and rain clutter controls to suit prevailing conditions
  Head up, North up mode

3   Understanding the picture:
* The factors affecting the clarity of the visual image

4 Radar reflectors
- Understanding what affects the received image

5 Fixing Position by radar
- Plot the vessel's position. Use of VRM and EBL

6 Pilotage by radar
- Understands how to prepare a simple pilotage plan including use of clearing ranges

7 Collision avoidance
- Understands how to determine the risk of collision with another vessel
- CPA, course and speed
- The existence of automatic radar plotting aids (ARPA & MARPA)
- The implications of IRPCS when in restricted visibility

You can keep a record of your achievements by attaching your course completion certificates in the following pages. It is important to keep your logbook and certificates in a safe place as the RYA does not keep a central record of course completion certificates issued.

Please note the difference between course completion certificates and Certificates of Competence.

CERTIFICATES OF COMPETENCE

RYA/MCA Coastal Skipper and RYA/MCA Yachtmaster® Certificates of Competence are only awarded after a successful practical assessment at sea.

RYA/MCA Yachtmaster® Ocean Certificates of Competence are awarded to holders of RYA/MCA Yachtmaster Offshore who have completed the theoretical and practical shore based examination and successfully complete an oral assessment.

The RYA maintains a record of holders of RYA/MCA Certificates of Competence.

PRACTICAL COURSE
START YACHTING

ATTACH YOUR CERTIFICATE HERE

Sailing – Competent Crew

CCPC

30086

PRACTICAL SAILING COURSE
Competent Crew

This is to certify that ......MAUREEN...BURGESS......

has attended a course of instruction at sea and demonstrated practical ability in all aspects of the syllabus for RYA Competent Crew.

Special endorsements ....

Signed .... *Date* .12.ᵗʰ.APRIL.2007

Principal / Chief Instructor

RYA *Training Centre* **Club Sail**
Sea School
Est. 1986

77

Course completion certificates

PRACTICAL COURSE
RYA/MCA COASTAL SKIPPER NON-TIDAL

ATTACH YOUR CERTIFICATE HERE

DS4

RYA/MCA Day Skipper for Sail & Power Craft

SHOREBASED COURSE
RYA/MCA Day Skipper for Sail & Power Craft

This is to certify that

MAUREEN BURGESS

*has attended a shorebased course of instruction and demonstrated a
knowledge of theory up to the standard of
RYA/MCA Day Skipper/Watch Leader*

Special Endorsements ....

Signed *Thomas H Mill* .... Date 9/2/08

YMOI   *Principal/Chief Instructor*

R/A *Training Centre*

ROYAL TAY YACHT CLUB

SHOREBASED COURSE
COASTAL SKIPPER AND YACHTMASTER OFFSHORE

ATTACH YOUR CERTIFICATE HERE

SHOREBASED COURSE
YACHTMASTER OCEAN

ATTACH YOUR CERTIFICATE HERE

There is no central record of course completion certificates.

SHOREBASED COURSE
FIRST AID

ATTACH YOUR CERTIFICATE HERE

SHOREBASED COURSE
RESTRICTED (VHF ONLY) RADIO

ATTACH YOUR CERTIFICATE HERE

SHOREBASED COURSE
DIESEL ENGINE

ATTACH YOUR CERTIFICATE HERE

PRACTICAL COURSE
RYA/MCA BASIC SEA SURVIVAL FOR SMALL CRAFT

ATTACH YOUR CERTIFICATE HERE

SHOREBASED COURSE
RYA RADAR

ATTACH YOUR CERTIFICATE HERE

NAME ..... MAUREEN BURGESS

ADDRESS ..... 2 KINLOCH STABLES
..... KINLOCH FARM
..... BY LADYBANK

CHANGE OF ADDRESS .....
.....
.....

RYA Membership

Promoting and Protecting Boating

The RYA is the national organisation which represents the interests of everyone who goes boating for pleasure.

The greater the membership, the louder our voice when it comes to protecting members' interests.

Apply for membership today, and support the RYA, to help the RYA support you.

Benefits of Membership

- Access to expert advice on all aspects of boating from legal wrangles to training matters
- Special members' discounts on a range of products and services including boat insurance, books, videos and class certificates
- Free issue of certificates of competence, increasingly asked for by everyone from overseas governments to holiday companies, insurance underwriters to boat hirers

- Access to the wide range of RYA publications, including the quarterly magazine
- Third Party insurance for windsurfing members
- Free Internet access with RYA-Online
- Special discounts on AA membership
- Regular offers in RYA Magazine
- ...and much more

Join now - membership form opposite

Join online at *www.rya.org.uk*

Visit our website for information, advice, members' services and web shop.